your whole life™ Journal

Carol Showalter
with Maggie Davis
MS, RD, LDN, FADA, CDE

Authors of *Your Whole Life*™
The 3D Plan for Eating Right, Living Well, and Loving God

THE 3D PLAN
EAT RIGHT • LIVE WELL • LOVE GOD
www.3DYourWholeLife.com

BREWSTER, MASSACHUSETTS

Your Whole Life™ Journal
2007 First Printing

Copyright © 2007 by Paraclete Press
Pages 184–189 copyright © 2007 by Maggie Davis

ISBN: 978-1-55725-581-5

10 9 8 7 6 5 4 3 2 1

Published by Paraclete Press
Brewster, Massachusetts
www.paracletepress.com
Printed in the United States of America

This Is Your Time...

REFLECT, REFLECT, REFLECT. Surely, these are three of the most important things you must do right now, and each day, from this day forward. If you are reading this, you have probably already read (or have begun to read) *Your Whole Life: The 3D Plan for Eating Right, Living Well, and Loving God*. As Maggie Davis and I make clear in *Your Whole Life*, the life change you are pursuing will not happen by simply reading a book. There's a lot more involved than just that. You need a support group of others around you. You need to pray and listen for God's voice. And you need to reflect.

Consider this journal your new companion, your new "best friend" with whom you should be completely honest. It is designed for a three-month journey in the 3D Plan and helps to reinforce the principles and advice in *Your Whole Life*. For twelve weeks in *Your Whole Life*, you will encounter daily Scripture verses and questions for reflection. The journal provides ample place for spiritual reflection, and offers an easy system for food journaling.

Set this journal on your bedside table, on the kitchen counter, or on your desk at work—wherever you are most likely to encounter it from day to day, throughout the day. Don't forget to spend time with your journal; doing so will remind you to spend time with God, as well as with yourself.

Ponder the Scripture verses; sit with them long enough each day to allow the words to stay with you the whole day long. Use the Scriptures as your springboard to reflecting honestly about what you are feeling as you work your way through the 3D program. This process takes work.

I encourage you to write down your thoughts during the day, and to make note of your worries and stress points. Coming to recognize where and why you feel pressure and anxiety is vitally important, and writing these things down will help you to realize the hold they may have on your life. Of course, you can share these same things with other people, but many of us can't do that every single day.

The daily food record couldn't be easier. You will simply follow the icons on the page and make a record of what you've eaten each day. Keep track of what you are missing in the different food categories. Just circle the number of servings you eat beside the food group shown. Please refer to the Food Groups charts and to the Recommended Daily Portion Guidelines found in the back of this journal. Remember, your goal is to learn how to eat right. Most of us are unaware of our habit patterns; checking off these categories will enlighten you and encourage you to adjust in different areas. You may even find it helpful to list each and every item you eat, in the space provided.

There is also a place to record the minutes you are exercising or the number of steps you are logging on your pedometer. This is also intended to make you more aware each day of exactly what you are doing. If you decide that you are not exercising enough, you can increase your exercise at your own pace in the days ahead.

Lastly, I encourage you to record your weight once a week in the space provided.

Your journal is an expression of who you are! Enjoy using it daily. And keep in touch with us. We'd love to hear from you at www.3DYourWholeLife.com, so that we can support you on this journey.

Yours truly,

Carol Showalter

your
whole
life ™
Journal

Vegetables 1 2 3 4 5 6 7 8 9 10

Fruits 1 2 3 4 5 6 7 8 9 10

Whole Grains 1 2 3 4 5 6 7 8 9 10

Starches 1 2 3 4 5 6 7 8 9 10

High Calcium Foods 1 2 3 4 5 6 7 8 9 10

High Protein Foods 1 2 3 4 5 6 7 8 9 10

Oils & Other Fats 1 2 3 4 5 6 7 8 9 10

Water 1 2 3 4 5 6 7 8 9 10

Other foods and
beverages _____

_____

■ Number of steps _____

■ Other exercise (minutes) _____

■ Did you read your Scripture and devotions today? Yes | No

■ Did you pray for others today? Yes | No

■ How did you "live well" today?

thoughts   needs   feelings

Be still, and know that I am God.
Psalm 46:10a

Vegetables 1 2 3 4 5 6 7 8 9 10

Fruits 1 2 3 4 5 6 7 8 9 10

Whole Grains 1 2 3 4 5 6 7 8 9 10

Starches 1 2 3 4 5 6 7 8 9 10

High Calcium Foods 1 2 3 4 5 6 7 8 9 10

High Protein Foods 1 2 3 4 5 6 7 8 9 10

Oils & Other Fats 1 2 3 4 5 6 7 8 9 10

Water 1 2 3 4 5 6 7 8 9 10

Other foods and beverages _____

_____

■ Number of steps _____

■ Other exercise (minutes) _____

■ Did you read your Scripture and devotions today? Yes | No

■ Did you pray for others today? Yes | No

■ How did you "live well" today?

thoughts   needs   feelings

Vegetables 1 2 3 4 5 6 7 8 9 10

Fruits 1 2 3 4 5 6 7 8 9 10

Whole Grains 1 2 3 4 5 6 7 8 9 10

Starches 1 2 3 4 5 6 7 8 9 10

High Calcium Foods 1 2 3 4 5 6 7 8 9 10

High Protein Foods 1 2 3 4 5 6 7 8 9 10

Oils & Other Fats 1 2 3 4 5 6 7 8 9 10

Water 1 2 3 4 5 6 7 8 9 10

Other foods and
beverages _____

_____

■ Number of steps _____

■ Other exercise (minutes) _____

■ Did you read your Scripture and devotions today? Yes | No

■ Did you pray for others today? Yes | No

■ How did you "live well" today?

thoughts   needs   feelings

Vegetables 1 2 3 4 5 6 7 8 9 10

Fruits 1 2 3 4 5 6 7 8 9 10

Whole Grains 1 2 3 4 5 6 7 8 9 10

Starches 1 2 3 4 5 6 7 8 9 10

High Calcium Foods 1 2 3 4 5 6 7 8 9 10

High Protein Foods 1 2 3 4 5 6 7 8 9 10

Oils & Other Fats 1 2 3 4 5 6 7 8 9 10

Water 1 2 3 4 5 6 7 8 9 10

Other foods and
beverages _____

_____

■ Number of steps _____

■ Other exercise (minutes) _____

■ Did you read your Scripture and devotions today? Yes | No

■ Did you pray for others today? Yes | No

■ How did you "live well" today?

thoughts   needs   feelings

week1 DAY 5   *date*

Vegetables 1 2 3 4 5 6 7 8 9 10

Fruits 1 2 3 4 5 6 7 8 9 10

Whole Grains 1 2 3 4 5 6 7 8 9 10

Starches 1 2 3 4 5 6 7 8 9 10

High Calcium Foods 1 2 3 4 5 6 7 8 9 10

High Protein Foods 1 2 3 4 5 6 7 8 9 10

Oils & Other Fats 1 2 3 4 5 6 7 8 9 10

Water 1 2 3 4 5 6 7 8 9 10

Other foods and
beverages _____

_____

Number of steps _____

Other exercise (minutes) _____

Did you read your Scripture and devotions today? Yes | No

Did you pray for others today? Yes | No

How did you "live well" today?

thoughts   needs   feelings

Vegetables 1 2 3 4 5 6 7 8 9 10

Fruits 1 2 3 4 5 6 7 8 9 10

Whole Grains 1 2 3 4 5 6 7 8 9 10

Starches 1 2 3 4 5 6 7 8 9 10

High Calcium Foods 1 2 3 4 5 6 7 8 9 10

High Protein Foods 1 2 3 4 5 6 7 8 9 10

Oils & Other Fats 1 2 3 4 5 6 7 8 9 10

Water 1 2 3 4 5 6 7 8 9 10

Other foods and
beverages _____

_____

Number of steps _____

Other exercise (minutes) _____

Did you read your Scripture and devotions today? Yes | No

Did you pray for others today? Yes | No

How did you "live well" today?

thoughts   needs   feelings

date

my weight

Vegetables 1 2 3 4 5 6 7 8 9 10

Fruits 1 2 3 4 5 6 7 8 9 10

Whole Grains 1 2 3 4 5 6 7 8 9 10

Starches 1 2 3 4 5 6 7 8 9 10

High Calcium Foods 1 2 3 4 5 6 7 8 9 10

High Protein Foods 1 2 3 4 5 6 7 8 9 10

Oils & Other Fats 1 2 3 4 5 6 7 8 9 10

Water 1 2 3 4 5 6 7 8 9 10

Other foods and
beverages _____

_____

Number of steps _____

Other exercise (minutes) _____

Did you read your Scripture and devotions today? Yes | No

Did you pray for others today? Yes | No

How did you "live well" today?

thoughts   needs   feelings

week2 DAY 1   *date*

Vegetables 1 2 3 4 5 6 7 8 9 10

Fruits 1 2 3 4 5 6 7 8 9 10

Whole Grains 1 2 3 4 5 6 7 8 9 10

Starches 1 2 3 4 5 6 7 8 9 10

High Calcium Foods 1 2 3 4 5 6 7 8 9 10

High Protein Foods 1 2 3 4 5 6 7 8 9 10

Oils & Other Fats 1 2 3 4 5 6 7 8 9 10

Water 1 2 3 4 5 6 7 8 9 10

Other foods and
beverages _____

_____

Number of steps _____

Other exercise (minutes) _____

Did you read your Scripture and devotions today? Yes | No

Did you pray for others today? Yes | No

How did you "live well" today?

For the moment all discipline seems painful rather than pleasant; later it yields the peaceful fruit of righteousness to those who have been trained by it.

Hebrews 12:11

Vegetables 1 2 3 4 5 6 7 8 9 10

Fruits 1 2 3 4 5 6 7 8 9 10

Whole Grains 1 2 3 4 5 6 7 8 9 10

Starches 1 2 3 4 5 6 7 8 9 10

High Calcium Foods 1 2 3 4 5 6 7 8 9 10

High Protein Foods 1 2 3 4 5 6 7 8 9 10

Oils & Other Fats 1 2 3 4 5 6 7 8 9 10

Water 1 2 3 4 5 6 7 8 9 10

Other foods and
beverages _____

_____

Number of steps _____

Other exercise (minutes) _____

Did you read your Scripture and devotions today? Yes | No

Did you pray for others today? Yes | No

How did you "live well" today?

thoughts   needs   feelings

Vegetables 1 2 3 4 5 6 7 8 9 10

Fruits 1 2 3 4 5 6 7 8 9 10

Whole Grains 1 2 3 4 5 6 7 8 9 10

Starches 1 2 3 4 5 6 7 8 9 10

High Calcium Foods 1 2 3 4 5 6 7 8 9 10

High Protein Foods 1 2 3 4 5 6 7 8 9 10

Oils & Other Fats 1 2 3 4 5 6 7 8 9 10

Water 1 2 3 4 5 6 7 8 9 10

Other foods and
beverages _____

_____

■ Number of steps _____

■ Other exercise (minutes) _____

■ Did you read your Scripture and devotions today? Yes | No

■ Did you pray for others today? Yes | No

■ How did you "live well" today?

thoughts   needs   feelings

Vegetables 1 2 3 4 5 6 7 8 9 10

Fruits 1 2 3 4 5 6 7 8 9 10

Whole Grains 1 2 3 4 5 6 7 8 9 10

Starches 1 2 3 4 5 6 7 8 9 10

High Calcium Foods 1 2 3 4 5 6 7 8 9 10

High Protein Foods 1 2 3 4 5 6 7 8 9 10

Oils & Other Fats 1 2 3 4 5 6 7 8 9 10

Water 1 2 3 4 5 6 7 8 9 10

Other foods and
beverages _____

_____

Number of steps _____

Other exercise (minutes) _____

Did you read your Scripture and devotions today? Yes | No

Did you pray for others today? Yes | No

How did you "live well" today?

thoughts   needs   feelings

Vegetables 1 2 3 4 5 6 7 8 9 10

Fruits 1 2 3 4 5 6 7 8 9 10

Whole Grains 1 2 3 4 5 6 7 8 9 10

Starches 1 2 3 4 5 6 7 8 9 10

High Calcium Foods 1 2 3 4 5 6 7 8 9 10

High Protein Foods 1 2 3 4 5 6 7 8 9 10

Oils & Other Fats 1 2 3 4 5 6 7 8 9 10

Water 1 2 3 4 5 6 7 8 9 10

Other foods and
beverages _____

_____

Number of steps _____

Other exercise (minutes) _____

Did you read your Scripture and devotions today? Yes | No

Did you pray for others today? Yes | No

How did you "live well" today?

thoughts   needs   feelings

Vegetables 1 2 3 4 5 6 7 8 9 10

Fruits 1 2 3 4 5 6 7 8 9 10

Whole Grains 1 2 3 4 5 6 7 8 9 10

Starches 1 2 3 4 5 6 7 8 9 10

High Calcium Foods 1 2 3 4 5 6 7 8 9 10

High Protein Foods 1 2 3 4 5 6 7 8 9 10

Oils & Other Fats 1 2 3 4 5 6 7 8 9 10

Water 1 2 3 4 5 6 7 8 9 10

Other foods and
beverages _____

_____

Number of steps _____

Other exercise (minutes) _____

Did you read your Scripture and devotions today? Yes | No

Did you pray for others today? Yes | No

How did you "live well" today?

thoughts   needs   feelings

week2 DAY 7

date

my weight

Vegetables 1 2 3 4 5 6 7 8 9 10

Fruits 1 2 3 4 5 6 7 8 9 10

Whole Grains 1 2 3 4 5 6 7 8 9 10

Starches 1 2 3 4 5 6 7 8 9 10

High Calcium Foods 1 2 3 4 5 6 7 8 9 10

High Protein Foods 1 2 3 4 5 6 7 8 9 10

Oils & Other Fats 1 2 3 4 5 6 7 8 9 10

Water 1 2 3 4 5 6 7 8 9 10

Other foods and
beverages _____

_____

■ Number of steps _____

■ Other exercise (minutes) _____

■ Did you read your Scripture and devotions today? Yes | No

■ Did you pray for others today? Yes | No

■ How did you "live well" today?

thoughts   needs   feelings

Vegetables 1 2 3 4 5 6 7 8 9 10

Fruits 1 2 3 4 5 6 7 8 9 10

Whole Grains 1 2 3 4 5 6 7 8 9 10

Starches 1 2 3 4 5 6 7 8 9 10

High Calcium Foods 1 2 3 4 5 6 7 8 9 10

High Protein Foods 1 2 3 4 5 6 7 8 9 10

Oils & Other Fats 1 2 3 4 5 6 7 8 9 10

Water 1 2 3 4 5 6 7 8 9 10

Other foods and
beverages _____

_____

Number of steps _____

Other exercise (minutes) _____

Did you read your Scripture and devotions today? Yes | No

Did you pray for others today? Yes | No

How did you "live well" today?

thoughts   needs   feelings

Nevertheless not my will, but thine, be done.
Luke 22:42

week3DAY2   *date*

Vegetables 1 2 3 4 5 6 7 8 9 10

Fruits 1 2 3 4 5 6 7 8 9 10

Whole Grains 1 2 3 4 5 6 7 8 9 10

Starches 1 2 3 4 5 6 7 8 9 10

High Calcium Foods 1 2 3 4 5 6 7 8 9 10

High Protein Foods 1 2 3 4 5 6 7 8 9 10

Oils & Other Fats 1 2 3 4 5 6 7 8 9 10

Water 1 2 3 4 5 6 7 8 9 10

Other foods and
beverages _____

_____

Number of steps _____

Other exercise (minutes) _____

Did you read your Scripture and devotions today? Yes | No

Did you pray for others today? Yes | No

How did you "live well" today?

thoughts   needs   feelings

Vegetables 1 2 3 4 5 6 7 8 9 10

Fruits 1 2 3 4 5 6 7 8 9 10

Whole Grains 1 2 3 4 5 6 7 8 9 10

Starches 1 2 3 4 5 6 7 8 9 10

High Calcium Foods 1 2 3 4 5 6 7 8 9 10

High Protein Foods 1 2 3 4 5 6 7 8 9 10

Oils & Other Fats 1 2 3 4 5 6 7 8 9 10

Water 1 2 3 4 5 6 7 8 9 10

Other foods and
beverages _____

_____

Number of steps _____

Other exercise (minutes) _____

Did you read your Scripture and devotions today? Yes | No

Did you pray for others today? Yes | No

How did you "live well" today?

thoughts   needs   feelings

week3DAY4   *date*

Vegetables 1 2 3 4 5 6 7 8 9 10

Fruits 1 2 3 4 5 6 7 8 9 10

Whole Grains 1 2 3 4 5 6 7 8 9 10

Starches 1 2 3 4 5 6 7 8 9 10

High Calcium Foods 1 2 3 4 5 6 7 8 9 10

High Protein Foods 1 2 3 4 5 6 7 8 9 10

Oils & Other Fats 1 2 3 4 5 6 7 8 9 10

Water 1 2 3 4 5 6 7 8 9 10

Other foods and
beverages _____

_____

Number of steps _____

Other exercise (minutes) _____

Did you read your Scripture and devotions today? Yes | No

Did you pray for others today? Yes | No

How did you "live well" today?

thoughts   needs   feelings

Vegetables 1 2 3 4 5 6 7 8 9 10

Fruits 1 2 3 4 5 6 7 8 9 10

Whole Grains 1 2 3 4 5 6 7 8 9 10

Starches 1 2 3 4 5 6 7 8 9 10

High Calcium Foods 1 2 3 4 5 6 7 8 9 10

High Protein Foods 1 2 3 4 5 6 7 8 9 10

Oils & Other Fats 1 2 3 4 5 6 7 8 9 10

Water 1 2 3 4 5 6 7 8 9 10

Other foods and
beverages _____

_____

▓ Number of steps _____

▓ Other exercise (minutes) _____

▓ Did you read your Scripture and devotions today? Yes | No

▓ Did you pray for others today? Yes | No

▓ How did you "live well" today?

thoughts   needs   feelings

week3DAY6   *date*

Vegetables 1 2 3 4 5 6 7 8 9 10

Fruits 1 2 3 4 5 6 7 8 9 10

Whole Grains 1 2 3 4 5 6 7 8 9 10

Starches 1 2 3 4 5 6 7 8 9 10

High Calcium Foods 1 2 3 4 5 6 7 8 9 10

High Protein Foods 1 2 3 4 5 6 7 8 9 10

Oils & Other Fats 1 2 3 4 5 6 7 8 9 10

Water 1 2 3 4 5 6 7 8 9 10

Other foods and
beverages _____

_____

Number of steps _____

Other exercise (minutes) _____

Did you read your Scripture and devotions today? Yes | No

Did you pray for others today? Yes | No

How did you "live well" today?

thoughts   needs   feelings

date

my weight

Vegetables 1 2 3 4 5 6 7 8 9 10

Fruits 1 2 3 4 5 6 7 8 9 10

Whole Grains 1 2 3 4 5 6 7 8 9 10

Starches 1 2 3 4 5 6 7 8 9 10

High Calcium Foods 1 2 3 4 5 6 7 8 9 10

High Protein Foods 1 2 3 4 5 6 7 8 9 10

Oils & Other Fats 1 2 3 4 5 6 7 8 9 10

Water 1 2 3 4 5 6 7 8 9 10

Other foods and
beverages _____

_____

Number of steps _____

Other exercise (minutes) _____

Did you read your Scripture and devotions today? Yes | No

Did you pray for others today? Yes | No

How did you "live well" today?

thoughts   needs   feelings

Vegetables 1 2 3 4 5 6 7 8 9 10

Fruits 1 2 3 4 5 6 7 8 9 10

Whole Grains 1 2 3 4 5 6 7 8 9 10

Starches 1 2 3 4 5 6 7 8 9 10

High Calcium Foods 1 2 3 4 5 6 7 8 9 10

High Protein Foods 1 2 3 4 5 6 7 8 9 10

Oils & Other Fats 1 2 3 4 5 6 7 8 9 10

Water 1 2 3 4 5 6 7 8 9 10

Other foods and
beverages _____

_____

▪ Number of steps _____

▪ Other exercise (minutes) _____

▪ Did you read your Scripture and devotions today? Yes | No

▪ Did you pray for others today? Yes | No

▪ How did you "live well" today?

thoughts   needs   feelings

But he who listens to me will dwell secure and will be at ease, without dread of evil.

Proverbs 1:33

week4 **DAY2**   *date*

Vegetables 1 2 3 4 5 6 7 8 9 10

Fruits 1 2 3 4 5 6 7 8 9 10

Whole Grains 1 2 3 4 5 6 7 8 9 10

Starches 1 2 3 4 5 6 7 8 9 10

High Calcium Foods 1 2 3 4 5 6 7 8 9 10

High Protein Foods 1 2 3 4 5 6 7 8 9 10

Oils & Other Fats 1 2 3 4 5 6 7 8 9 10

Water 1 2 3 4 5 6 7 8 9 10

Other foods and
beverages _____

_____

Number of steps _____

Other exercise (minutes) _____

Did you read your Scripture and devotions today? Yes | No

Did you pray for others today? Yes | No

How did you "live well" today?

thoughts   needs   feelings

week4**DAY3**   *d a t e*

Vegetables 1 2 3 4 5 6 7 8 9 10

Fruits 1 2 3 4 5 6 7 8 9 10

Whole Grains 1 2 3 4 5 6 7 8 9 10

Starches 1 2 3 4 5 6 7 8 9 10

High Calcium Foods 1 2 3 4 5 6 7 8 9 10

High Protein Foods 1 2 3 4 5 6 7 8 9 10

Oils & Other Fats 1 2 3 4 5 6 7 8 9 10

Water 1 2 3 4 5 6 7 8 9 10

Other foods and
beverages _____

_____

■ Number of steps _____

■ Other exercise (minutes) _____

■ Did you read your Scripture and devotions today? Yes | No

■ Did you pray for others today? Yes | No

■ How did you "live well" today?

thoughts   needs   feelings

Vegetables 1 2 3 4 5 6 7 8 9 10

Fruits 1 2 3 4 5 6 7 8 9 10

Whole Grains 1 2 3 4 5 6 7 8 9 10

Starches 1 2 3 4 5 6 7 8 9 10

High Calcium Foods 1 2 3 4 5 6 7 8 9 10

High Protein Foods 1 2 3 4 5 6 7 8 9 10

Oils & Other Fats 1 2 3 4 5 6 7 8 9 10

Water 1 2 3 4 5 6 7 8 9 10

Other foods and
beverages _____

_____

■ Number of steps _____

■ Other exercise (minutes) _____

■ Did you read your Scripture and devotions today? Yes | No

■ Did you pray for others today? Yes | No

■ How did you "live well" today?

thoughts   needs   feelings

date

Vegetables 1 2 3 4 5 6 7 8 9 10

Fruits 1 2 3 4 5 6 7 8 9 10

Whole Grains 1 2 3 4 5 6 7 8 9 10

Starches 1 2 3 4 5 6 7 8 9 10

High Calcium Foods 1 2 3 4 5 6 7 8 9 10

High Protein Foods 1 2 3 4 5 6 7 8 9 10

Oils & Other Fats 1 2 3 4 5 6 7 8 9 10

Water 1 2 3 4 5 6 7 8 9 10

Other foods and
beverages _____

_____

■ Number of steps _____

■ Other exercise (minutes) _____

■ Did you read your Scripture and devotions today? Yes | No

■ Did you pray for others today? Yes | No

■ How did you "live well" today?

thoughts   needs   feelings

week4DAY6 *date*

Vegetables 1 2 3 4 5 6 7 8 9 10

Fruits 1 2 3 4 5 6 7 8 9 10

Whole Grains 1 2 3 4 5 6 7 8 9 10

Starches 1 2 3 4 5 6 7 8 9 10

High Calcium Foods 1 2 3 4 5 6 7 8 9 10

High Protein Foods 1 2 3 4 5 6 7 8 9 10

Oils & Other Fats 1 2 3 4 5 6 7 8 9 10

Water 1 2 3 4 5 6 7 8 9 10

Other foods and
beverages _____

_____

Number of steps _____

Other exercise (minutes) _____

Did you read your Scripture and devotions today? Yes | No

Did you pray for others today? Yes | No

How did you "live well" today?

thoughts   needs   feelings

date

my weight

Vegetables 1 2 3 4 5 6 7 8 9 10

Fruits 1 2 3 4 5 6 7 8 9 10

Whole Grains 1 2 3 4 5 6 7 8 9 10

Starches 1 2 3 4 5 6 7 8 9 10

High Calcium Foods 1 2 3 4 5 6 7 8 9 10

High Protein Foods 1 2 3 4 5 6 7 8 9 10

Oils & Other Fats 1 2 3 4 5 6 7 8 9 10

Water 1 2 3 4 5 6 7 8 9 10

Other foods and
beverages _____

_____

■ Number of steps _____

■ Other exercise (minutes) _____

■ Did you read your Scripture and devotions today? Yes | No

■ Did you pray for others today? Yes | No

■ How did you "live well" today?

thoughts   needs   feelings

Vegetables 1 2 3 4 5 6 7 8 9 10

Fruits 1 2 3 4 5 6 7 8 9 10

Whole Grains 1 2 3 4 5 6 7 8 9 10

Starches 1 2 3 4 5 6 7 8 9 10

High Calcium Foods 1 2 3 4 5 6 7 8 9 10

High Protein Foods 1 2 3 4 5 6 7 8 9 10

Oils & Other Fats 1 2 3 4 5 6 7 8 9 10

Water 1 2 3 4 5 6 7 8 9 10

Other foods and
beverages _____

_____

Number of steps _____

Other exercise (minutes) _____

Did you read your Scripture and devotions today? Yes | No

Did you pray for others today? Yes | No

How did you "live well" today?

*He who has my commandments and keeps them,
he it is who loves me; and he who loves me will be loved by my Father,
and I will love him and manifest myself to him.*

John 14:21

week5**DAY2**   *date*

Vegetables 1 2 3 4 5 6 7 8 9 10

Fruits 1 2 3 4 5 6 7 8 9 10

Whole Grains 1 2 3 4 5 6 7 8 9 10

Starches 1 2 3 4 5 6 7 8 9 10

High Calcium Foods 1 2 3 4 5 6 7 8 9 10

High Protein Foods 1 2 3 4 5 6 7 8 9 10

Oils & Other Fats 1 2 3 4 5 6 7 8 9 10

Water 1 2 3 4 5 6 7 8 9 10

Other foods and
beverages _____

_____

■ Number of steps _____

■ Other exercise (minutes) _____

■ Did you read your Scripture and devotions today? Yes | No

■ Did you pray for others today? Yes | No

■ How did you "live well" today?

thoughts   needs   feelings

Vegetables 1 2 3 4 5 6 7 8 9 10

Fruits 1 2 3 4 5 6 7 8 9 10

Whole Grains 1 2 3 4 5 6 7 8 9 10

Starches 1 2 3 4 5 6 7 8 9 10

High Calcium Foods 1 2 3 4 5 6 7 8 9 10

High Protein Foods 1 2 3 4 5 6 7 8 9 10

Oils & Other Fats 1 2 3 4 5 6 7 8 9 10

Water 1 2 3 4 5 6 7 8 9 10

Other foods and
beverages _____

_____

■ Number of steps _____

■ Other exercise (minutes) _____

■ Did you read your Scripture and devotions today? Yes | No

■ Did you pray for others today? Yes | No

■ How did you "live well" today?

thoughts   needs   feelings

date

Vegetables 1 2 3 4 5 6 7 8 9 10

Fruits 1 2 3 4 5 6 7 8 9 10

Whole Grains 1 2 3 4 5 6 7 8 9 10

Starches 1 2 3 4 5 6 7 8 9 10

High Calcium Foods 1 2 3 4 5 6 7 8 9 10

High Protein Foods 1 2 3 4 5 6 7 8 9 10

Oils & Other Fats 1 2 3 4 5 6 7 8 9 10

Water 1 2 3 4 5 6 7 8 9 10

Other foods and beverages _____

_____

■ Number of steps _____

■ Other exercise (minutes) _____

■ Did you read your Scripture and devotions today? Yes | No

■ Did you pray for others today? Yes | No

■ How did you "live well" today?

thoughts   needs   feelings

Vegetables 1 2 3 4 5 6 7 8 9 10

Fruits 1 2 3 4 5 6 7 8 9 10

Whole Grains 1 2 3 4 5 6 7 8 9 10

Starches 1 2 3 4 5 6 7 8 9 10

High Calcium Foods 1 2 3 4 5 6 7 8 9 10

High Protein Foods 1 2 3 4 5 6 7 8 9 10

Oils & Other Fats 1 2 3 4 5 6 7 8 9 10

Water 1 2 3 4 5 6 7 8 9 10

Other foods and
beverages _____

_____

Number of steps _____

Other exercise (minutes) _____

Did you read your Scripture and devotions today? Yes | No

Did you pray for others today? Yes | No

How did you "live well" today?

thoughts   needs   feelings

Vegetables 1 2 3 4 5 6 7 8 9 10

Fruits 1 2 3 4 5 6 7 8 9 10

Whole Grains 1 2 3 4 5 6 7 8 9 10

Starches 1 2 3 4 5 6 7 8 9 10

High Calcium Foods 1 2 3 4 5 6 7 8 9 10

High Protein Foods 1 2 3 4 5 6 7 8 9 10

Oils & Other Fats 1 2 3 4 5 6 7 8 9 10

Water 1 2 3 4 5 6 7 8 9 10

Other foods and
beverages _____

_____

■ Number of steps _____

■ Other exercise (minutes) _____

■ Did you read your Scripture and devotions today? Yes | No

■ Did you pray for others today? Yes | No

■ How did you "live well" today?

thoughts   needs   feelings

week5DAY7

Vegetables 1 2 3 4 5 6 7 8 9 10

Fruits 1 2 3 4 5 6 7 8 9 10

Whole Grains 1 2 3 4 5 6 7 8 9 10

Starches 1 2 3 4 5 6 7 8 9 10

High Calcium Foods 1 2 3 4 5 6 7 8 9 10

High Protein Foods 1 2 3 4 5 6 7 8 9 10

Oils & Other Fats 1 2 3 4 5 6 7 8 9 10

Water 1 2 3 4 5 6 7 8 9 10

Other foods and
beverages _____

_____

Number of steps _____

Other exercise (minutes) _____

Did you read your Scripture and devotions today? Yes | No

Did you pray for others today? Yes | No

How did you "live well" today?

thoughts   needs   feelings

Vegetables 1 2 3 4 5 6 7 8 9 10

Fruits 1 2 3 4 5 6 7 8 9 10

Whole Grains 1 2 3 4 5 6 7 8 9 10

Starches 1 2 3 4 5 6 7 8 9 10

High Calcium Foods 1 2 3 4 5 6 7 8 9 10

High Protein Foods 1 2 3 4 5 6 7 8 9 10

Oils & Other Fats 1 2 3 4 5 6 7 8 9 10

Water 1 2 3 4 5 6 7 8 9 10

Other foods and
   beverages _____

_____

Number of steps _____

Other exercise (minutes) _____

Did you read your Scripture and devotions today? Yes | No

Did you pray for others today? Yes | No

How did you "live well" today?

Behold, to obey is better than sacrifice,
and to hearken than the fat of rams.
For rebellion is as the sin of witchcraft,
and stubbornness is as iniquity and idolatry.
1 Samuel 15:22b, 23 (KJV)

week6DAY2   *date*

Vegetables 1 2 3 4 5 6 7 8 9 10

Fruits 1 2 3 4 5 6 7 8 9 10

Whole Grains 1 2 3 4 5 6 7 8 9 10

Starches 1 2 3 4 5 6 7 8 9 10

High Calcium Foods 1 2 3 4 5 6 7 8 9 10

High Protein Foods 1 2 3 4 5 6 7 8 9 10

Oils & Other Fats 1 2 3 4 5 6 7 8 9 10

Water 1 2 3 4 5 6 7 8 9 10

Other foods and
beverages _____

_____

Number of steps _____

Other exercise (minutes) _____

Did you read your Scripture and devotions today? Yes | No

Did you pray for others today? Yes | No

How did you "live well" today?

thoughts   needs   feelings

Vegetables 1 2 3 4 5 6 7 8 9 10

Fruits 1 2 3 4 5 6 7 8 9 10

Whole Grains 1 2 3 4 5 6 7 8 9 10

Starches 1 2 3 4 5 6 7 8 9 10

High Calcium Foods 1 2 3 4 5 6 7 8 9 10

High Protein Foods 1 2 3 4 5 6 7 8 9 10

Oils & Other Fats 1 2 3 4 5 6 7 8 9 10

Water 1 2 3 4 5 6 7 8 9 10

Other foods and
beverages _____

_____

■ Number of steps _____

■ Other exercise (minutes) _____

■ Did you read your Scripture and devotions today? Yes | No

■ Did you pray for others today? Yes | No

■ How did you "live well" today?

thoughts   needs   feelings

week6DAY4 *date*

Vegetables 1 2 3 4 5 6 7 8 9 10

Fruits 1 2 3 4 5 6 7 8 9 10

Whole Grains 1 2 3 4 5 6 7 8 9 10

Starches 1 2 3 4 5 6 7 8 9 10

High Calcium Foods 1 2 3 4 5 6 7 8 9 10

High Protein Foods 1 2 3 4 5 6 7 8 9 10

Oils & Other Fats 1 2 3 4 5 6 7 8 9 10

Water 1 2 3 4 5 6 7 8 9 10

Other foods and beverages _____

_____

Number of steps _____

Other exercise (minutes) _____

Did you read your Scripture and devotions today? Yes | No

Did you pray for others today? Yes | No

How did you "live well" today?

thoughts   needs   feelings

week6DAY5   *date*

Vegetables 1 2 3 4 5 6 7 8 9 10

Fruits 1 2 3 4 5 6 7 8 9 10

Whole Grains 1 2 3 4 5 6 7 8 9 10

Starches 1 2 3 4 5 6 7 8 9 10

High Calcium Foods 1 2 3 4 5 6 7 8 9 10

High Protein Foods 1 2 3 4 5 6 7 8 9 10

Oils & Other Fats 1 2 3 4 5 6 7 8 9 10

Water 1 2 3 4 5 6 7 8 9 10

Other foods and
beverages _____

_____

■ Number of steps _____

■ Other exercise (minutes) _____

■ Did you read your Scripture and devotions today? Yes | No

■ Did you pray for others today? Yes | No

■ How did you "live well" today?

thoughts   needs   feelings

Vegetables 1 2 3 4 5 6 7 8 9 10

Fruits 1 2 3 4 5 6 7 8 9 10

Whole Grains 1 2 3 4 5 6 7 8 9 10

Starches 1 2 3 4 5 6 7 8 9 10

High Calcium Foods 1 2 3 4 5 6 7 8 9 10

High Protein Foods 1 2 3 4 5 6 7 8 9 10

Oils & Other Fats 1 2 3 4 5 6 7 8 9 10

Water 1 2 3 4 5 6 7 8 9 10

Other foods and
beverages _____

_____

■ Number of steps _____

■ Other exercise (minutes) _____

■ Did you read your Scripture and devotions today? Yes | No

■ Did you pray for others today? Yes | No

■ How did you "live well" today?

thoughts   needs   feelings

date

my weight

Vegetables 1 2 3 4 5 6 7 8 9 10

Fruits 1 2 3 4 5 6 7 8 9 10

Whole Grains 1 2 3 4 5 6 7 8 9 10

Starches 1 2 3 4 5 6 7 8 9 10

High Calcium Foods 1 2 3 4 5 6 7 8 9 10

High Protein Foods 1 2 3 4 5 6 7 8 9 10

Oils & Other Fats 1 2 3 4 5 6 7 8 9 10

Water 1 2 3 4 5 6 7 8 9 10

Other foods and
 beverages _____

_____

■ Number of steps _____

■ Other exercise (minutes) _____

■ Did you read your Scripture and devotions today? Yes | No

■ Did you pray for others today? Yes | No

■ How did you "live well" today?

thoughts   needs   feelings

Vegetables 1 2 3 4 5 6 7 8 9 10

Fruits 1 2 3 4 5 6 7 8 9 10

Whole Grains 1 2 3 4 5 6 7 8 9 10

Starches 1 2 3 4 5 6 7 8 9 10

High Calcium Foods 1 2 3 4 5 6 7 8 9 10

High Protein Foods 1 2 3 4 5 6 7 8 9 10

Oils & Other Fats 1 2 3 4 5 6 7 8 9 10

Water 1 2 3 4 5 6 7 8 9 10

Other foods and
beverages _____

_____

Number of steps _____

Other exercise (minutes) _____

Did you read your Scripture and devotions today? Yes | No

Did you pray for others today? Yes | No

How did you "live well" today?

For the Lord disciplines him whom he loves,
and chastises every son whom he receives.

Hebrews 12:6

Vegetables 1 2 3 4 5 6 7 8 9 10

Fruits 1 2 3 4 5 6 7 8 9 10

Whole Grains 1 2 3 4 5 6 7 8 9 10

Starches 1 2 3 4 5 6 7 8 9 10

High Calcium Foods 1 2 3 4 5 6 7 8 9 10

High Protein Foods 1 2 3 4 5 6 7 8 9 10

Oils & Other Fats 1 2 3 4 5 6 7 8 9 10

Water 1 2 3 4 5 6 7 8 9 10

Other foods and
beverages _____

_____

■ Number of steps _____

■ Other exercise (minutes) _____

■ Did you read your Scripture and devotions today? Yes | No

■ Did you pray for others today? Yes | No

■ How did you "live well" today?

thoughts   needs   feelings

Vegetables 1 2 3 4 5 6 7 8 9 10

Fruits 1 2 3 4 5 6 7 8 9 10

Whole Grains 1 2 3 4 5 6 7 8 9 10

Starches 1 2 3 4 5 6 7 8 9 10

High Calcium Foods 1 2 3 4 5 6 7 8 9 10

High Protein Foods 1 2 3 4 5 6 7 8 9 10

Oils & Other Fats 1 2 3 4 5 6 7 8 9 10

Water 1 2 3 4 5 6 7 8 9 10

Other foods and
   beverages _____

   _____

■ Number of steps _____

■ Other exercise (minutes) _____

■ Did you read your Scripture and devotions today? Yes | No

■ Did you pray for others today? Yes | No

■ How did you "live well" today?

thoughts   needs   feelings

Vegetables 1 2 3 4 5 6 7 8 9 10

Fruits 1 2 3 4 5 6 7 8 9 10

Whole Grains 1 2 3 4 5 6 7 8 9 10

Starches 1 2 3 4 5 6 7 8 9 10

High Calcium Foods 1 2 3 4 5 6 7 8 9 10

High Protein Foods 1 2 3 4 5 6 7 8 9 10

Oils & Other Fats 1 2 3 4 5 6 7 8 9 10

Water 1 2 3 4 5 6 7 8 9 10

Other foods and
beverages _____

_____

■ Number of steps _____

■ Other exercise (minutes) _____

■ Did you read your Scripture and devotions today? Yes | No

■ Did you pray for others today? Yes | No

■ How did you "live well" today?

thoughts   needs   feelings

Vegetables 1 2 3 4 5 6 7 8 9 10

Fruits 1 2 3 4 5 6 7 8 9 10

Whole Grains 1 2 3 4 5 6 7 8 9 10

Starches 1 2 3 4 5 6 7 8 9 10

High Calcium Foods 1 2 3 4 5 6 7 8 9 10

High Protein Foods 1 2 3 4 5 6 7 8 9 10

Oils & Other Fats 1 2 3 4 5 6 7 8 9 10

Water 1 2 3 4 5 6 7 8 9 10

Other foods and
beverages _____

_____

Number of steps _____

Other exercise (minutes) _____

Did you read your Scripture and devotions today? Yes | No

Did you pray for others today? Yes | No

How did you "live well" today?

thoughts   needs   feelings

Vegetables   1 2 3 4 5 6 7 8 9 10

Fruits   1 2 3 4 5 6 7 8 9 10

Whole Grains   1 2 3 4 5 6 7 8 9 10

Starches   1 2 3 4 5 6 7 8 9 10

High Calcium Foods   1 2 3 4 5 6 7 8 9 10

High Protein Foods   1 2 3 4 5 6 7 8 9 10

Oils & Other Fats   1 2 3 4 5 6 7 8 9 10

Water   1 2 3 4 5 6 7 8 9 10

Other foods and
beverages _____

_____

■ Number of steps _____

■ Other exercise (minutes) _____

■ Did you read your Scripture and devotions today? Yes | No

■ Did you pray for others today? Yes | No

■ How did you "live well" today?

thoughts   needs   feelings

date

my weight

Vegetables 1 2 3 4 5 6 7 8 9 10

Fruits 1 2 3 4 5 6 7 8 9 10

Whole Grains 1 2 3 4 5 6 7 8 9 10

Starches 1 2 3 4 5 6 7 8 9 10

High Calcium Foods 1 2 3 4 5 6 7 8 9 10

High Protein Foods 1 2 3 4 5 6 7 8 9 10

Oils & Other Fats 1 2 3 4 5 6 7 8 9 10

Water 1 2 3 4 5 6 7 8 9 10

Other foods and
beverages _____

_____

■ Number of steps _____

■ Other exercise (minutes) _____

■ Did you read your Scripture and devotions today? Yes | No

■ Did you pray for others today? Yes | No

■ How did you "live well" today?

thoughts   needs   feelings

week8DAY1 *date*

Vegetables 1 2 3 4 5 6 7 8 9 10

Fruits 1 2 3 4 5 6 7 8 9 10

Whole Grains 1 2 3 4 5 6 7 8 9 10

Starches 1 2 3 4 5 6 7 8 9 10

High Calcium Foods 1 2 3 4 5 6 7 8 9 10

High Protein Foods 1 2 3 4 5 6 7 8 9 10

Oils & Other Fats 1 2 3 4 5 6 7 8 9 10

Water 1 2 3 4 5 6 7 8 9 10

Other foods and
beverages _____

_____

Number of steps _____

Other exercise (minutes) _____

Did you read your Scripture and devotions today? Yes | No

Did you pray for others today? Yes | No

How did you "live well" today?

thoughts   needs   feelings

*If we confess our sins, he is faithful and just,
and will forgive our sins and cleanse us from all unrighteousness.*

1 John 1:9

week8DAY2   *date*

Vegetables 1 2 3 4 5 6 7 8 9 10

Fruits 1 2 3 4 5 6 7 8 9 10

Whole Grains 1 2 3 4 5 6 7 8 9 10

Starches 1 2 3 4 5 6 7 8 9 10

High Calcium Foods 1 2 3 4 5 6 7 8 9 10

High Protein Foods 1 2 3 4 5 6 7 8 9 10

Oils & Other Fats 1 2 3 4 5 6 7 8 9 10

Water 1 2 3 4 5 6 7 8 9 10

Other foods and
beverages _____

_____

Number of steps _____

Other exercise (minutes) _____

Did you read your Scripture and devotions today? Yes | No

Did you pray for others today? Yes | No

How did you "live well" today?

thoughts   needs   feelings

week8DAY3

Vegetables 1 2 3 4 5 6 7 8 9 10

Fruits 1 2 3 4 5 6 7 8 9 10

Whole Grains 1 2 3 4 5 6 7 8 9 10

Starches 1 2 3 4 5 6 7 8 9 10

High Calcium Foods 1 2 3 4 5 6 7 8 9 10

High Protein Foods 1 2 3 4 5 6 7 8 9 10

Oils & Other Fats 1 2 3 4 5 6 7 8 9 10

Water 1 2 3 4 5 6 7 8 9 10

Other foods and
beverages _____

_____

- Number of steps _____

- Other exercise (minutes) _____

- Did you read your Scripture and devotions today? Yes | No

- Did you pray for others today? Yes | No

- How did you "live well" today?

thoughts   needs   feelings

Vegetables 1 2 3 4 5 6 7 8 9 10

Fruits 1 2 3 4 5 6 7 8 9 10

Whole Grains 1 2 3 4 5 6 7 8 9 10

Starches 1 2 3 4 5 6 7 8 9 10

High Calcium Foods 1 2 3 4 5 6 7 8 9 10

High Protein Foods 1 2 3 4 5 6 7 8 9 10

Oils & Other Fats 1 2 3 4 5 6 7 8 9 10

Water 1 2 3 4 5 6 7 8 9 10

Other foods and
beverages _____

_____

■ Number of steps _____

■ Other exercise (minutes) _____

■ Did you read your Scripture and devotions today? Yes | No

■ Did you pray for others today? Yes | No

■ How did you "live well" today?

thoughts   needs   feelings

Vegetables 1 2 3 4 5 6 7 8 9 10

Fruits 1 2 3 4 5 6 7 8 9 10

Whole Grains 1 2 3 4 5 6 7 8 9 10

Starches 1 2 3 4 5 6 7 8 9 10

High Calcium Foods 1 2 3 4 5 6 7 8 9 10

High Protein Foods 1 2 3 4 5 6 7 8 9 10

Oils & Other Fats 1 2 3 4 5 6 7 8 9 10

Water 1 2 3 4 5 6 7 8 9 10

Other foods and
beverages _____

_____

Number of steps _____

Other exercise (minutes) _____

Did you read your Scripture and devotions today? Yes | No

Did you pray for others today? Yes | No

How did you "live well" today?

thoughts   needs   feelings

date

Vegetables 1 2 3 4 5 6 7 8 9 10

Fruits 1 2 3 4 5 6 7 8 9 10

Whole Grains 1 2 3 4 5 6 7 8 9 10

Starches 1 2 3 4 5 6 7 8 9 10

High Calcium Foods 1 2 3 4 5 6 7 8 9 10

High Protein Foods 1 2 3 4 5 6 7 8 9 10

Oils & Other Fats 1 2 3 4 5 6 7 8 9 10

Water 1 2 3 4 5 6 7 8 9 10

Other foods and
beverages _____

_____

▧ Number of steps _____

▧ Other exercise (minutes) _____

▧ Did you read your Scripture and devotions today? Yes | No

▧ Did you pray for others today? Yes | No

▧ How did you "live well" today?

thoughts   needs   feelings

date

my weight

Vegetables 1 2 3 4 5 6 7 8 9 10

Fruits 1 2 3 4 5 6 7 8 9 10

Whole Grains 1 2 3 4 5 6 7 8 9 10

Starches 1 2 3 4 5 6 7 8 9 10

High Calcium Foods 1 2 3 4 5 6 7 8 9 10

High Protein Foods 1 2 3 4 5 6 7 8 9 10

Oils & Other Fats 1 2 3 4 5 6 7 8 9 10

Water 1 2 3 4 5 6 7 8 9 10

Other foods and
beverages _____

_____

Number of steps _____

Other exercise (minutes) _____

Did you read your Scripture and devotions today? Yes | No

Did you pray for others today? Yes | No

How did you "live well" today?

thoughts   needs   feelings

date

Vegetables 1 2 3 4 5 6 7 8 9 10

Fruits 1 2 3 4 5 6 7 8 9 10

Whole Grains 1 2 3 4 5 6 7 8 9 10

Starches 1 2 3 4 5 6 7 8 9 10

High Calcium Foods 1 2 3 4 5 6 7 8 9 10

High Protein Foods 1 2 3 4 5 6 7 8 9 10

Oils & Other Fats 1 2 3 4 5 6 7 8 9 10

Water 1 2 3 4 5 6 7 8 9 10

Other foods and
beverages _____

_____

Number of steps _____

Other exercise (minutes) _____

Did you read your Scripture and devotions today? Yes | No

Did you pray for others today? Yes | No

How did you "live well" today?

Rejoice with those who rejoice, weep with those who weep.

Romans 12:15

date

Vegetables 1 2 3 4 5 6 7 8 9 10

Fruits 1 2 3 4 5 6 7 8 9 10

Whole Grains 1 2 3 4 5 6 7 8 9 10

Starches 1 2 3 4 5 6 7 8 9 10

High Calcium Foods 1 2 3 4 5 6 7 8 9 10

High Protein Foods 1 2 3 4 5 6 7 8 9 10

Oils & Other Fats 1 2 3 4 5 6 7 8 9 10

Water 1 2 3 4 5 6 7 8 9 10

Other foods and
beverages _____

_____

Number of steps _____

Other exercise (minutes) _____

Did you read your Scripture and devotions today? Yes | No

Did you pray for others today? Yes | No

How did you "live well" today?

thoughts   needs   feelings

Vegetables 1 2 3 4 5 6 7 8 9 10

Fruits 1 2 3 4 5 6 7 8 9 10

Whole Grains 1 2 3 4 5 6 7 8 9 10

Starches 1 2 3 4 5 6 7 8 9 10

High Calcium Foods 1 2 3 4 5 6 7 8 9 10

High Protein Foods 1 2 3 4 5 6 7 8 9 10

Oils & Other Fats 1 2 3 4 5 6 7 8 9 10

Water 1 2 3 4 5 6 7 8 9 10

Other foods and
beverages _____

_____

Number of steps _____

Other exercise (minutes) _____

Did you read your Scripture and devotions today? Yes | No

Did you pray for others today? Yes | No

How did you "live well" today?

thoughts   needs   feelings

week9**DAY4**   *d a t e*

Vegetables 1 2 3 4 5 6 7 8 9 10

Fruits 1 2 3 4 5 6 7 8 9 10

Whole Grains 1 2 3 4 5 6 7 8 9 10

Starches 1 2 3 4 5 6 7 8 9 10

High Calcium Foods 1 2 3 4 5 6 7 8 9 10

High Protein Foods 1 2 3 4 5 6 7 8 9 10

Oils & Other Fats 1 2 3 4 5 6 7 8 9 10

Water 1 2 3 4 5 6 7 8 9 10

Other foods and
beverages _____

_____

Number of steps _____

Other exercise (minutes) _____

Did you read your Scripture and devotions today? Yes | No

Did you pray for others today? Yes | No

How did you "live well" today?

thoughts   needs   feelings

week9**DAY5**   *date*

Vegetables 1 2 3 4 5 6 7 8 9 10

Fruits 1 2 3 4 5 6 7 8 9 10

Whole Grains 1 2 3 4 5 6 7 8 9 10

Starches 1 2 3 4 5 6 7 8 9 10

High Calcium Foods 1 2 3 4 5 6 7 8 9 10

High Protein Foods 1 2 3 4 5 6 7 8 9 10

Oils & Other Fats 1 2 3 4 5 6 7 8 9 10

Water 1 2 3 4 5 6 7 8 9 10

Other foods and
beverages _____

_____

Number of steps _____

Other exercise (minutes) _____

Did you read your Scripture and devotions today? Yes | No

Did you pray for others today? Yes | No

How did you "live well" today?

thoughts   needs   feelings

Vegetables 1 2 3 4 5 6 7 8 9 10

Fruits 1 2 3 4 5 6 7 8 9 10

Whole Grains 1 2 3 4 5 6 7 8 9 10

Starches 1 2 3 4 5 6 7 8 9 10

High Calcium Foods 1 2 3 4 5 6 7 8 9 10

High Protein Foods 1 2 3 4 5 6 7 8 9 10

Oils & Other Fats 1 2 3 4 5 6 7 8 9 10

Water 1 2 3 4 5 6 7 8 9 10

Other foods and
beverages _____

_____

Number of steps _____

Other exercise (minutes) _____

Did you read your Scripture and devotions today? Yes | No

Did you pray for others today? Yes | No

How did you "live well" today?

thoughts   needs   feelings

week9**DAY7**

date

my weight

Vegetables 1 2 3 4 5 6 7 8 9 10

Fruits 1 2 3 4 5 6 7 8 9 10

Whole Grains 1 2 3 4 5 6 7 8 9 10

Starches 1 2 3 4 5 6 7 8 9 10

High Calcium Foods 1 2 3 4 5 6 7 8 9 10

High Protein Foods 1 2 3 4 5 6 7 8 9 10

Oils & Other Fats 1 2 3 4 5 6 7 8 9 10

Water 1 2 3 4 5 6 7 8 9 10

Other foods and
beverages _____

_____

Number of steps _____

Other exercise (minutes) _____

Did you read your Scripture and devotions today? Yes | No

Did you pray for others today? Yes | No

How did you "live well" today?

thoughts   needs   feelings

Vegetables 1 2 3 4 5 6 7 8 9 10

Fruits 1 2 3 4 5 6 7 8 9 10

Whole Grains 1 2 3 4 5 6 7 8 9 10

Starches 1 2 3 4 5 6 7 8 9 10

High Calcium Foods 1 2 3 4 5 6 7 8 9 10

High Protein Foods 1 2 3 4 5 6 7 8 9 10

Oils & Other Fats 1 2 3 4 5 6 7 8 9 10

Water 1 2 3 4 5 6 7 8 9 10

Other foods and
beverages _____

_____

■ Number of steps _____

■ Other exercise (minutes) _____

■ Did you read your Scripture and devotions today? Yes | No

■ Did you pray for others today? Yes | No

■ How did you "live well" today?

thoughts   needs   feelings

You will know the truth, and the truth will make you free.

John 8:32

Vegetables 1 2 3 4 5 6 7 8 9 10

Fruits 1 2 3 4 5 6 7 8 9 10

Whole Grains 1 2 3 4 5 6 7 8 9 10

Starches 1 2 3 4 5 6 7 8 9 10

High Calcium Foods 1 2 3 4 5 6 7 8 9 10

High Protein Foods 1 2 3 4 5 6 7 8 9 10

Oils & Other Fats 1 2 3 4 5 6 7 8 9 10

Water 1 2 3 4 5 6 7 8 9 10

Other foods and
beverages _____

_____

■ Number of steps _____

■ Other exercise (minutes) _____

■ Did you read your Scripture and devotions today? Yes | No

■ Did you pray for others today? Yes | No

■ How did you "live well" today?

thoughts   needs   feelings

week10**DAY3**   *date*

Vegetables 1 2 3 4 5 6 7 8 9 10

Fruits 1 2 3 4 5 6 7 8 9 10

Whole Grains 1 2 3 4 5 6 7 8 9 10

Starches 1 2 3 4 5 6 7 8 9 10

High Calcium Foods 1 2 3 4 5 6 7 8 9 10

High Protein Foods 1 2 3 4 5 6 7 8 9 10

Oils & Other Fats 1 2 3 4 5 6 7 8 9 10

Water 1 2 3 4 5 6 7 8 9 10

Other foods and
beverages _____

_____

■ Number of steps _____

■ Other exercise (minutes) _____

■ Did you read your Scripture and devotions today? Yes | No

■ Did you pray for others today? Yes | No

■ How did you "live well" today?

thoughts   needs   feelings

Vegetables 1 2 3 4 5 6 7 8 9 10

Fruits 1 2 3 4 5 6 7 8 9 10

Whole Grains 1 2 3 4 5 6 7 8 9 10

Starches 1 2 3 4 5 6 7 8 9 10

High Calcium Foods 1 2 3 4 5 6 7 8 9 10

High Protein Foods 1 2 3 4 5 6 7 8 9 10

Oils & Other Fats 1 2 3 4 5 6 7 8 9 10

Water 1 2 3 4 5 6 7 8 9 10

Other foods and
beverages _____

_____

■ Number of steps _____

■ Other exercise (minutes) _____

■ Did you read your Scripture and devotions today? Yes | No

■ Did you pray for others today? Yes | No

■ How did you "live well" today?

thoughts   needs   feelings

Vegetables 1 2 3 4 5 6 7 8 9 10

Fruits 1 2 3 4 5 6 7 8 9 10

Whole Grains 1 2 3 4 5 6 7 8 9 10

Starches 1 2 3 4 5 6 7 8 9 10

High Calcium Foods 1 2 3 4 5 6 7 8 9 10

High Protein Foods 1 2 3 4 5 6 7 8 9 10

Oils & Other Fats 1 2 3 4 5 6 7 8 9 10

Water 1 2 3 4 5 6 7 8 9 10

Other foods and
beverages _____

_____

- Number of steps _____

- Other exercise (minutes) _____

- Did you read your Scripture and devotions today? Yes | No

- Did you pray for others today? Yes | No

- How did you "live well" today?

thoughts   needs   feelings

Vegetables 1 2 3 4 5 6 7 8 9 10

Fruits 1 2 3 4 5 6 7 8 9 10

Whole Grains 1 2 3 4 5 6 7 8 9 10

Starches 1 2 3 4 5 6 7 8 9 10

High Calcium Foods 1 2 3 4 5 6 7 8 9 10

High Protein Foods 1 2 3 4 5 6 7 8 9 10

Oils & Other Fats 1 2 3 4 5 6 7 8 9 10

Water 1 2 3 4 5 6 7 8 9 10

Other foods and
beverages _____

_____

■ Number of steps _____

■ Other exercise (minutes) _____

■ Did you read your Scripture and devotions today? Yes | No

■ Did you pray for others today? Yes | No

■ How did you "live well" today?

thoughts   needs   feelings

week10DAY7

date

my weight

Vegetables 1 2 3 4 5 6 7 8 9 10

Fruits 1 2 3 4 5 6 7 8 9 10

Whole Grains 1 2 3 4 5 6 7 8 9 10

Starches 1 2 3 4 5 6 7 8 9 10

High Calcium Foods 1 2 3 4 5 6 7 8 9 10

High Protein Foods 1 2 3 4 5 6 7 8 9 10

Oils & Other Fats 1 2 3 4 5 6 7 8 9 10

Water 1 2 3 4 5 6 7 8 9 10

Other foods and
beverages _____

_____

Number of steps _____

Other exercise (minutes) _____

Did you read your Scripture and devotions today? Yes | No

Did you pray for others today? Yes | No

How did you "live well" today?

thoughts   needs   feelings

week11 DAY1

date

Vegetables 1 2 3 4 5 6 7 8 9 10

Fruits 1 2 3 4 5 6 7 8 9 10

Whole Grains 1 2 3 4 5 6 7 8 9 10

Starches 1 2 3 4 5 6 7 8 9 10

High Calcium Foods 1 2 3 4 5 6 7 8 9 10

High Protein Foods 1 2 3 4 5 6 7 8 9 10

Oils & Other Fats 1 2 3 4 5 6 7 8 9 10

Water 1 2 3 4 5 6 7 8 9 10

Other foods and
beverages _____

_____

Number of steps _____

Other exercise (minutes) _____

Did you read your Scripture and devotions today? Yes | No

Did you pray for others today? Yes | No

How did you "live well" today?

thoughts   needs   feelings

We destroy arguments and every proud obstacle to the knowledge of God,
and take every thought captive to obey Christ.

2 Corinthians 10:5

week11 DAY2

date

Vegetables 1 2 3 4 5 6 7 8 9 10

Fruits 1 2 3 4 5 6 7 8 9 10

Whole Grains 1 2 3 4 5 6 7 8 9 10

Starches 1 2 3 4 5 6 7 8 9 10

High Calcium Foods 1 2 3 4 5 6 7 8 9 10

High Protein Foods 1 2 3 4 5 6 7 8 9 10

Oils & Other Fats 1 2 3 4 5 6 7 8 9 10

Water 1 2 3 4 5 6 7 8 9 10

Other foods and beverages _____

_____

■ Number of steps _____

■ Other exercise (minutes) _____

■ Did you read your Scripture and devotions today? Yes | No

■ Did you pray for others today? Yes | No

■ How did you "live well" today?

thoughts   needs   feelings

week11 DAY3　　　*date*

Vegetables 1 2 3 4 5 6 7 8 9 10

Fruits 1 2 3 4 5 6 7 8 9 10

Whole Grains 1 2 3 4 5 6 7 8 9 10

Starches 1 2 3 4 5 6 7 8 9 10

High Calcium Foods 1 2 3 4 5 6 7 8 9 10

High Protein Foods 1 2 3 4 5 6 7 8 9 10

Oils & Other Fats 1 2 3 4 5 6 7 8 9 10

Water 1 2 3 4 5 6 7 8 9 10

Other foods and
beverages _____

_____

Number of steps _____

Other exercise (minutes) _____

Did you read your Scripture and devotions today? Yes | No

Did you pray for others today? Yes | No

How did you "live well" today?

thoughts   needs   feelings

Vegetables 1 2 3 4 5 6 7 8 9 10

Fruits 1 2 3 4 5 6 7 8 9 10

Whole Grains 1 2 3 4 5 6 7 8 9 10

Starches 1 2 3 4 5 6 7 8 9 10

High Calcium Foods 1 2 3 4 5 6 7 8 9 10

High Protein Foods 1 2 3 4 5 6 7 8 9 10

Oils & Other Fats 1 2 3 4 5 6 7 8 9 10

Water 1 2 3 4 5 6 7 8 9 10

Other foods and
beverages _____

_____

■ Number of steps _____

■ Other exercise (minutes) _____

■ Did you read your Scripture and devotions today? Yes | No

■ Did you pray for others today? Yes | No

■ How did you "live well" today?

thoughts   needs   feelings

Vegetables 1 2 3 4 5 6 7 8 9 10

Fruits 1 2 3 4 5 6 7 8 9 10

Whole Grains 1 2 3 4 5 6 7 8 9 10

Starches 1 2 3 4 5 6 7 8 9 10

High Calcium Foods 1 2 3 4 5 6 7 8 9 10

High Protein Foods 1 2 3 4 5 6 7 8 9 10

Oils & Other Fats 1 2 3 4 5 6 7 8 9 10

Water 1 2 3 4 5 6 7 8 9 10

Other foods and
beverages _____

_____

Number of steps _____

Other exercise (minutes) _____

Did you read your Scripture and devotions today? Yes | No

Did you pray for others today? Yes | No

How did you "live well" today?

thoughts   needs   feelings

week11 **DAY6**   *date*

Vegetables 1 2 3 4 5 6 7 8 9 10

Fruits 1 2 3 4 5 6 7 8 9 10

Whole Grains 1 2 3 4 5 6 7 8 9 10

Starches 1 2 3 4 5 6 7 8 9 10

High Calcium Foods 1 2 3 4 5 6 7 8 9 10

High Protein Foods 1 2 3 4 5 6 7 8 9 10

Oils & Other Fats 1 2 3 4 5 6 7 8 9 10

Water 1 2 3 4 5 6 7 8 9 10

Other foods and
beverages _____

_____

▓ Number of steps _____

▓ Other exercise (minutes) _____

▓ Did you read your Scripture and devotions today? Yes | No

▓ Did you pray for others today? Yes | No

▓ How did you "live well" today?

thoughts   needs   feelings

week11 DAY7

date

my weight

Vegetables 1 2 3 4 5 6 7 8 9 10

Fruits 1 2 3 4 5 6 7 8 9 10

Whole Grains 1 2 3 4 5 6 7 8 9 10

Starches 1 2 3 4 5 6 7 8 9 10

High Calcium Foods 1 2 3 4 5 6 7 8 9 10

High Protein Foods 1 2 3 4 5 6 7 8 9 10

Oils & Other Fats 1 2 3 4 5 6 7 8 9 10

Water 1 2 3 4 5 6 7 8 9 10

Other foods and
beverages _____

_____

■ Number of steps _____

■ Other exercise (minutes) _____

■ Did you read your Scripture and devotions today? Yes | No

■ Did you pray for others today? Yes | No

■ How did you "live well" today?

thoughts   needs   feelings

Vegetables 1 2 3 4 5 6 7 8 9 10

Fruits 1 2 3 4 5 6 7 8 9 10

Whole Grains 1 2 3 4 5 6 7 8 9 10

Starches 1 2 3 4 5 6 7 8 9 10

High Calcium Foods 1 2 3 4 5 6 7 8 9 10

High Protein Foods 1 2 3 4 5 6 7 8 9 10

Oils & Other Fats 1 2 3 4 5 6 7 8 9 10

Water 1 2 3 4 5 6 7 8 9 10

Other foods and beverages _____

_____

■ Number of steps _____

■ Other exercise (minutes) _____

■ Did you read your Scripture and devotions today? Yes | No

■ Did you pray for others today? Yes | No

■ How did you "live well" today?

thoughts   needs   feelings

If any man will come after me, let him deny himself and take up his cross daily and follow me.

Luke 9:23

Vegetables 1 2 3 4 5 6 7 8 9 10

Fruits 1 2 3 4 5 6 7 8 9 10

Whole Grains 1 2 3 4 5 6 7 8 9 10

Starches 1 2 3 4 5 6 7 8 9 10

High Calcium Foods 1 2 3 4 5 6 7 8 9 10

High Protein Foods 1 2 3 4 5 6 7 8 9 10

Oils & Other Fats 1 2 3 4 5 6 7 8 9 10

Water 1 2 3 4 5 6 7 8 9 10

Other foods and
beverages _____

_____

■ Number of steps _____

■ Other exercise (minutes) _____

■ Did you read your Scripture and devotions today? Yes | No

■ Did you pray for others today? Yes | No

■ How did you "live well" today?

thoughts   needs   feelings

Vegetables 1 2 3 4 5 6 7 8 9 10

Fruits 1 2 3 4 5 6 7 8 9 10

Whole Grains 1 2 3 4 5 6 7 8 9 10

Starches 1 2 3 4 5 6 7 8 9 10

High Calcium Foods 1 2 3 4 5 6 7 8 9 10

High Protein Foods 1 2 3 4 5 6 7 8 9 10

Oils & Other Fats 1 2 3 4 5 6 7 8 9 10

Water 1 2 3 4 5 6 7 8 9 10

Other foods and
beverages _____

_____

◼ Number of steps _____

◼ Other exercise (minutes) _____

◼ Did you read your Scripture and devotions today? Yes | No

◼ Did you pray for others today? Yes | No

◼ How did you "live well" today?

thoughts   needs   feelings

Vegetables 1 2 3 4 5 6 7 8 9 10

Fruits 1 2 3 4 5 6 7 8 9 10

Whole Grains 1 2 3 4 5 6 7 8 9 10

Starches 1 2 3 4 5 6 7 8 9 10

High Calcium Foods 1 2 3 4 5 6 7 8 9 10

High Protein Foods 1 2 3 4 5 6 7 8 9 10

Oils & Other Fats 1 2 3 4 5 6 7 8 9 10

Water 1 2 3 4 5 6 7 8 9 10

Other foods and
beverages _____

_____

■ Number of steps _____

■ Other exercise (minutes) _____

■ Did you read your Scripture and devotions today? Yes | No

■ Did you pray for others today? Yes | No

■ How did you "live well" today?

thoughts   needs   feelings

week12**DAY5**   *d a t e*

Vegetables 1 2 3 4 5 6 7 8 9 10

Fruits 1 2 3 4 5 6 7 8 9 10

Whole Grains 1 2 3 4 5 6 7 8 9 10

Starches 1 2 3 4 5 6 7 8 9 10

High Calcium Foods 1 2 3 4 5 6 7 8 9 10

High Protein Foods 1 2 3 4 5 6 7 8 9 10

Oils & Other Fats 1 2 3 4 5 6 7 8 9 10

Water 1 2 3 4 5 6 7 8 9 10

Other foods and
beverages _____

_____

Number of steps _____

Other exercise (minutes) _____

Did you read your Scripture and devotions today? Yes | No

Did you pray for others today? Yes | No

How did you "live well" today?

thoughts   needs   feelings

week12 DAY6   *date*

Vegetables 1 2 3 4 5 6 7 8 9 10

Fruits 1 2 3 4 5 6 7 8 9 10

Whole Grains 1 2 3 4 5 6 7 8 9 10

Starches 1 2 3 4 5 6 7 8 9 10

High Calcium Foods 1 2 3 4 5 6 7 8 9 10

High Protein Foods 1 2 3 4 5 6 7 8 9 10

Oils & Other Fats 1 2 3 4 5 6 7 8 9 10

Water 1 2 3 4 5 6 7 8 9 10

Other foods and
beverages _____

_____

■ Number of steps _____

■ Other exercise (minutes) _____

■ Did you read your Scripture and devotions today? Yes | No

■ Did you pray for others today? Yes | No

■ How did you "live well" today?

thoughts   needs   feelings

d a t e

my weight

Vegetables 1 2 3 4 5 6 7 8 9 10

Fruits 1 2 3 4 5 6 7 8 9 10

Whole Grains 1 2 3 4 5 6 7 8 9 10

Starches 1 2 3 4 5 6 7 8 9 10

High Calcium Foods 1 2 3 4 5 6 7 8 9 10

High Protein Foods 1 2 3 4 5 6 7 8 9 10

Oils & Other Fats 1 2 3 4 5 6 7 8 9 10

Water 1 2 3 4 5 6 7 8 9 10

Other foods and
beverages _____

_____

Number of steps _____

Other exercise (minutes) _____

Did you read your Scripture and devotions today? Yes | No

Did you pray for others today? Yes | No

How did you "live well" today?

thoughts   needs   feelings

The Next Step
of the Journey

Things that have meant the most to me

New things I have learned about myself

Memory verses I now know by heart

Things I have learned about eating right

Things I have learned about living well

Things I have learned about loving God

The next steps for me

Food Groups and Portion Sizes

Vegetables (1 cup raw or 1/2 cup cooked)

artichokes	endive	radishes
arugula	escarole	romaine
asparagus	green beans	rutabaga
bamboo shoots	kale	scallions
bean sprouts	kohlrabi	spinach
beets	leeks	summer squash
bok choy	lettuce (any variety)	tomatillos
broccoli	mesclun	tomatoes
Broccolini	mushrooms	turnip greens
Brussells sprouts	mustard greens	turnips
cabbage	okra	watercress
carrots	onions	water chestnuts
cauliflower	parsnips	wax beans
celery	pea pods	winter squash
collard greens	peppers (any color)	zucchini
cucumbers	pumpkin	
eggplant	raddichio	

Fruits

apples, 1 small	4 oz	limes	1
apricots, dried	8 halves	mangoes, half of a small fruit	1/2 cup
banana, 1/2 large	4 oz	melons (any kind)	1 cup
berries	1 cup	nectarines, 1 small	5 oz
cherries, 12	3 oz	oranges, 1 small	6 oz
clementines, 2 small	8 oz	peaches, 1 medium	6 oz
dried fruit without added sugar	1/4 cup	pears, 1 small or 1/2 large	4 oz
fresh figs, 2 medium	3 oz	plums (dried)	3
grapefruit half	11 oz	plums (fresh), 2 small	5 oz
grapefruit sections	1/2 cup	raisins	2 Tbsp
grapes (any color) 12-18	3 oz	tangerines, 2 small	8 oz
kiwi, 1	3.5 oz	watermelon	1 cup
lemons	1		

Whole Grains

brown or wild rice, cooked	1/3 cup
buckwheat flour	3 Tbsp
buckwheat groats	2 Tbsp
bulghur (cracked wheat)	1/2 cup
Kamut grain	2 Tbsp
oat bran breads	1.5 oz
oatmeal, cooked	1/2 cup
popcorn, unbuttered	3 cups
quinoa, uncooked	2 Tbsp
spelt flour	3 Tbsp
spelt grain	2 Tbsp
sprouted grain breads and rolls	1 oz
whole grain amaranth	2 Tbsp
whole grain barley, cooked	1/3 cup
whole grain corn meal	3 Tbsp
whole grain crackers	3/4 oz
whole grain rye or wheat bread	1 oz
whole grain sorghum	2 Tbsp
whole grain triticale	2 Tbsp
whole grain wheat flake cereal	3/4 cup
whole wheat flour	3 Tbsp
whole wheat pasta	1/3 cup
whole wheat pita, 6 inch	1/2 slice

Starches & Starchy Vegetables

Starches (Refined Grains)

bagel	1/5th
cold cereal, unsweetened	3/4 cup
cornstarch	2 Tbsp
Cream of Wheat or Rice	1/2 cup
croutons	1 cup
English muffin	1/2
flour	3 Tbsp
grits	1/2 cup
hummus	1/3 cup
matzoh	3/4 oz
non-whole grain breads	1 oz
pancake or waffle, 4 inch	1
pasta or couscous	1/3 cup
pita bread, 6 inch	1/2 slice
popcorn, unbuttered	3 cups
pretzels	3/4 oz
puffed wheat or rice	1.5 cups
reduced calorie breads	1.5 oz
rice cakes	2
Ritz crackers	6
saltine-type crackers	6
snack chips	3/4 oz
stuffing	1/3 cup
tortilla, 6 inch	1
white rice	1/3

Starchy Vegetables

baked beans	1/3 cup
baked potato, 1/4 large	1/2 cup
corn	1/2 cup or 1/2 cob
peas	1/2 cup
plantain	1/2 cup
potatoes, boiled	1/2 cup
sweet potato	2/3 cup
winter squash	3 oz
yam	1/2 cup

High Calcium Foods

buttermilk	1 cup
collard greens, cooked	1 cup
desserts made with milk or yogurt*	1 cup
evaporated milk	1 cup
fat-free dry milk powder	1 cup
goat's milk	1/3 cup
kefir, unsweetened	1 cup
low-lactose or lactose-free milk	1 cup
lowfat hard cheese, shredded	1/3 cup
lowfat hard cheese	1.5 oz
nonfat or lowfat milk	1 cup
nonfat or lowfat yogurt	1 cup
ricotta, low fat	1/2 cup
soy beverages	
fortified with calcium	1 cup
spinach	1 cup

when choosing these foods, use the extra Calories as part of your personal choice Calories

Lean High Protein Foods
lean unprocessed animal protein:

lean beef (such as choice or select grades of round, sirloin, tenderloin, flank steak)	1 oz
chicken (white or dark meat without skin)	1 oz
eggs	1
egg substitutes	1/4 cup
egg whites	1
fish, ocean or fresh water fish	1 oz
ground meats (less than 10% fat content)	1 oz
lamb	1 oz
pork	1 oz
shellfish	1 oz
turkey (white or dark meat without skin)	1 oz
veal	1 oz
venison	1 oz
game meats (without skin—goose, duck, rabbit)	1 oz
lowfat or fat-free cottage cheese	1/4 cup
grated parmesan	2 Tbsp
fat-free cheese	1 oz
oysters	1 oz
sardines (canned, drained)	6

Lean High Protein Foods
vegetable protein sources:

black beans (cooked or canned)	1/2 cup
black-eyed peas	
(cooked or canned)	1/2 cup
chickpeas (garbanzo beans)	1/2 cup
falafel	1/2 cup
kidney beans, red or white	
(cooked or canned)	1/2 cup
lentils (cooked)	1/2 cup
navy beans (cooked or canned)	1/3 cup
nuts	1/2 cup
pinto beans	2 Tbsp
Quorn	1/2 cup
seeds	1 oz
soy beans, roasted	2 Tbsp
Soy beans shelled, edamame	2 Tbsp
soy meats	1 oz patty
tempeh	1 oz
tofu	1/4 cup
white beans	
(cooked or canned)	1/2 cup

Highly Unsaturated Fats & Oils

avocado oil	1 tsp
avocados	2 Tbsp
canola oil	1 tsp
fatty fish	
(such as anchovies, salmon,	
sardines)	1/2 oz
grape seed oil	1 tsp
low fat mayonnaise	1 Tbsp
nut butters	2 tsp
nuts	1 Tbsp
olive oil (preferably extra virgin,	
cold pressed)	1 tsp
olives	9
peanut oil (for stir-frying)	1 tsp
salad dressing (olive oil based)	1 Tbsp
seeds (pumpkin, sesame,	
sunflower)	1 Tbsp
sesame oil	1 tsp
sesame tahini	2 tsp
walnut oil	1 tsp

Other Foods & Beverages

alcoholic beverages
butter, cream, sour cream
candy
cookies
cured meats
ice cream
jams & jellies
juices
pastries
shortening or lard
snack foods
sodas and sweetened beverages
sports drinks
sugars & syrups
sweets & desserts

Recommended Daily Portion Guidelines

food group	calories/serving	800	1000	1200	1400
Vegetables	25-50	2	2	3	3
Fruits	80	1	1	1	1.5
Whole Grains	80	2	3	3	3
Starches	80	0	0	0	1
High Calcium Foods	100	1.5	1.5	2	2
High Protein Foods	60-100	3	3	4	4
Oils & Other Fats	50	1	2	3	4
Water (8 oz)	0	5	5	6	6

		800	1000	1200	1400
Core Food Calories		705	835	1035	1205
Your Choice Calories		100	150	175	175
Total Calories		805	985	1210	1380

1600	1800	2000	2200	2400	2600	2800	3000
3	3	3	4	4	4	5	5
1.5	2	2	2	2	2	2.5	2.5
3	3	3	3	4	5	5	5
1	2	3	4	4	4	4	5
3	3	3	3	3	3	3	3
5	6	6	6	7	7	7	7
5	5	6	7	7	8	9	10
7	7	8	8	9	9	10	10

1420	1605	1735	1900	2045	2175	2295	2425
175	200	250	300	350	400	500	550
1595	1805	1985	2200	2395	2575	2795	2975

The 3D Prayer

Dear Lord,
This is a new day
That means I can expect from your hand
    all I need to live.
Help me to know
Your grace is sufficient
Your power is overwhelming
    and your peace and joy are here for the asking.
I need you in so many practical ways, Lord
I need you to help me choose the right spirit
    at the beginning of the day
I need you to help me with my family
    the work I need to get done
    and the pressures that come at me
    before my eyes are even open.
I need you to go ahead of me every step of the way
You will do that
This day is yours
I am yours.
Thank you for loving me and giving me
    the gift of life today.
When I am ready to close my eyes
    at the end of this day
May I say with a steady voice:
I have loved you more today than I did yesterday
But not as much as I will tomorrow.
Make it so, dear Lord.
Amen.

Must-have Companions
on Your Journey to Wholeness

Your Whole Life™ PEDOMETER

Clip this little tool to your waistband or hip pocket and let it become part of your daily discipline. | $12.95

Your Whole Life™ INSPIRATIONAL CD

Get inspired by a message from Carol Showalter—one for each of the twelve weeks. This engaging, 36-minute CD is also ideal for playing aloud at your weekly meetings. | $16.95

The 3D PRAYER CARD

"Dear Lord, This is a new day. . . ." A personal prayer by Carol Showalter, beautifully designed and laminated. Available in packs of 10. | $4.95/pack

THE 3D PLAN
EAT RIGHT • LIVE WELL • LOVE GOD

For more information, go to the 3D website,
www.3DYourWholeLife.com, or call 1-800-451-5006.